ULEY DURSLEY & CAM
THROUGH TIME

Alan Sutton

AMBERLEY PUBLISHING

The Churchyard Gate circa 1865

First published 2008

Amberley Publishing Plc
Cirencester Road, Chalford,
Stroud, Gloucestershire, GL6 8PE

www.amberley-books.com

British Library Cataloguing in Publication Data.
A catalogue record for this book is available from the British Library.

ISBN 978 1 84868 021 0

Typesetting and Origination by diagrafmedia
Printed in Great Britain by Amberley Publishing

Introduction

Producing this book has been a harder task than I imagined it would be when I set forth on the project in the Spring. To begin with, taking the colour photographs during the worst summer in recorded history has been a challenge. This difficulty has been compounded by tree growth and by new housing, as many of the views that were photographed in the years around 1900-1905 are impossible to take now due to increased tree cover and general development.

These problems aside, perhaps the biggest challenge has been to decide what to include in this short volume. After much agonising, chopping and changing, I have finally come up with a selection which I hope is of interest to those living in the Ewelme and River Cam Valley.

I have tried to provide as many unpublished images as possible, but inevitably there is repetition and many of the finer pictures have already appeared in earlier photograph books on Dursley. I have made the selection with the specific aim of providing good comparisons against the modern views.

Dursley is currently on the verge of a change. After a painful adjustment to a post-industrial era, the town will hopefully look forward to a brighter future. This book provides a focus on the industrial heritage and the unfortunate mess that past industries have left behind for us. Since the heyday of the 1950s, R. A. Lister & Company went into decline in the 1970s and the dwindling remnants struggle to survive. Mawdsleys moved from Uley Road to Gloucester, seemingly to decline and die. Now the sites of both companies are either houses, or destined to be houses. In fact, this increasing development in Dursley is a surprise to me. Perhaps the biggest shock I have experienced in returning to photograph the home town of my childhood is the change in the Union Street and Hunger Hill area. I was aware of the development at Sutton Close, the site once covered by my grandparents' garden, but to see the houses on the site of the Workhouse and in May Lane forcibly emphasised the pace of change in the twenty-first century.

In 1991, some seventeen years into my publishing career, I published *Uley, Dursley and Cam in Old Photographs*. 'Old Photographs' was a growing series in my publishing company, but the Dursley book was a 'first', for it heralded a new design and a new concept, with the front cover being produced in a rich sepia tone. Unfortunately the book was badly printed by the Bath Press, but nevertheless, the sepia-toned series has gone on (and still goes on) with more than 10,000 titles having been published in the UK, USA, France, Germany and Belgium — all spawned from the first Dursley book. Now, with this title we have another first, for the 'Through Time' series marks a radical change in publishing style, with the use of full colour throughout the book.

To produce a new series, to be rolled out in many thousands of titles throughout the Western world, required some bench-mark testing and, yet again, Dursley has been the *beta* site. I needed first-hand experience regarding the problems encountered by authors when putting a book like this together, and the only way to gain such knowledge was to produce a test book — and here it is! The results of this work will now get written up in a new booklet, 'Notes to Authors'.

Undertaking this work has been an interesting experience for me. I can only hope that it is an interesting read for the residents of Uley, Dursley and Cam.

Finally, I must record my thanks for the loan of photographs and help given by Matt Welsh, Ashley Wood, Roger Wood and John Morris.

Alan Sutton

The Market House
The town centre destruction commences. The demolition of the old Police Station and Magistrates' Court, 1959.

Uley from Owlpen Lane
When I first tried to photograph this view I was thwarted by bad light, but met a friendly farmer driving a tractor towards me in the lane. When I went back on a better day, the same gentleman greeted me (this time on foot), telling me this viewpoint was a favourite for photographs. I should have asked his name, for his cheery conversation brightened my day. I have purposely not cropped my friend from the picture.

Looking down from The Green
This is one of the earliest views of Uley. The date of 1865-70 is suggested by the ladies' crinolines, fashionable from 1856 onwards. Note the late seventeenth-century house to the right of the Church, long since demolished. By the size of the central ground floor window it appears to have been a shop, probably that of Llewellyn Smith, grocer, draper and tailor. The landlord of the Old Crown was George Powell, who also doubled as a farmer.

The Green

A Red and White bus at the Old Crown, *c*.1938. Red Bus started in the early 1920s, when former Australian airman 'Dick' Reyne began bus service operations in this area. In 1933 Red Bus had sold to the growing and predominantly South Wales Red and White conglomerate, and Reyne transferred to the board of Red and White and continued his interest in bus operation for some years. Red and White disappeared in 1948 when bus services were nationalised. Note the cottage and out-houses jutting out into what is now the roadway.

The Lower Crown

It seems strange that two pubs, almost next door to one-another should both be called 'The Crown'. It is even more strange that one should choose to adopt the name 'Lower Crown', as if implying it is inferior! Obviously in elevation it was lower, and presumably that was the justification for the name. This view is from *c*.1947. The pub had been known as the Lower Crown for many years. In 1876 the landlord was George Baglin who was also a wood turner.

The Old Post Office

Not a great deal has changed in the last 100 years. The building to the right is no longer The Post Office, but in 1876 it advertised itself thus: 'Post Office and Postal Telegraph Office — George Ford, Jun., Postmaster. Letters delivered at 8.15 a.m. Money orders granted and paid, and savings bank and annuity business transacted, from 9 a.m. to 6 p.m.'

The Lamb Inn
This has long since ceased to be a pub. The other major change is in relation to the width of the street. The house to the left has gone and the roadway is now considerably wider than this view of *c.*1910.

Street Farm
Apart from the width and surface of the road, little appears to have changed in the street.
Chimneys have become shorter and the ivy has gone from Street Farm, otherwise little alteration.

The Turnpike

Travelling in the nineteenth century was not cheap. The tolls to be paid to pass through each tollgate were set out in an Act of Parliament. For each horse drawing a stagecoach or wagon the charge was likely to be in the region of eight pence, unless the fellies of the wheels were less than six inches in width, when it might be a shilling. The narrower the wheels the more the surface could be cut up. Any vehicle drawn by 'steam, gas or machinery' might pay up to two shillings.

Return journeys within 24 hours would be free. Needless to say attempts were made to avoid payment! If price inflation is at a ratio of 1 to 200 from 1800 to 2008, this might mean that a trip to Dursley in a horse and trap, or similar, would be the modern equivalent of £10. Turnpike houses very often had this three-sided front for the gatekeeper to have good vision of approaching traffic.

Uley from the West

These two photographs of Uley show views one hundred years apart. Note the general increase in tree cover. From the woodlands, and especially Uley Bury, the tree-line is creeping into the fields. The hedgerows are also more tree-filled.

Whiteway

These views are taken from Whiteway by the Reservoir. Again, note the increase in tree cover. This is currently the furthest eastern extremity of housing in Dursley. In the top photograph the house lies on one of the old, pre-turnpike roads to Uley, running via Sheepcote Farm. Another, more ancient route ran along what is now the bottom of Bowcote wood to Shadwell and Elcombe.

The Beginning of the Housing Explosion

The exact modern equivalent of this view is impossible due to tree growth on Whiteway Hill. My new photograph is taken about 100m to the south, above the Reservoir. The date must be 1936 as much of Highfields is in existence, but the new Lister Foundry is not yet built. Note the Gas Works at Trolleymoors smoking in the valley background.

Looking Towards Ferney Hill and Chestal
This view is probably about 1934 as Rosebery Park is not yet built. Note Rangers House, centre left, and Ferney Hill in the distance. This photograph was taken from higher up in the woodlands, slightly to the south east, but a comparable view is impossible due to tree growth.

The Old Nursery Gardens

A glimpse of the corner of the nursery gardens c.1915. The gardens were started in the mid-nineteenth century by Robert Smith; they then passed to the Morse family and later to Brinicombe and Son. When closed, the site was used for vehicle maintenance by J. H. Grange & Son, and later became Cousins's Garage. It no longer vends fuel and new houses are springing up with one under construction in the view below.

Woodmancote

A little further down Woodmancote in the late 1930s. The street scene here is remarkably unchanged with the exception of Fort Lane Cottage which was demolished in 1968. On the right-hand side, out of view, the story is different, with the Vizard Almshouses being long gone.

Vizard Almshouses

The Almshouses were built in 1858 and endowed by Henry Vizard to accommodate three old men and three old women. The buildings were demolished in 1968. The photograph here dates from c.1905.

The Bull Inn

Two views of the top of Bull Pitch, the top photograph *c.*1905 and the bottom one about twenty years later. The Bull Inn gave its name to Bull Pitch, but was closed in the early 1930s.

Bull Pitch
This photograph c.1960 was taken shortly after the magnificent Monkey Puzzle tree which stood in front of Dragon House was felled.

Silver Street

A view from Silver Street looking into Bull Pitch, *c.*1910 showing the Monkey Puzzle tree in situ. Bottom picture: the aftermath of the great snow of 1963. The winter of 1962-63 was exceptionally cold and the River Thames froze over. One particularly heavy snowfall on 10 January 1963 cut Dursley off for more than 24 hours. This photograph was taken about three days later.

Union Street circa 1905

My grandparents' house to the far left. This house, Hill View, was the scene of one of Dursley's most violent murders. Here on the night of Saturday 6 August 1859 Ellen Rutter slit her husband Thomas's throat with his own cut-throat razor. He was a wife beater and kept the razor under his pillow to threaten her. That evening they had both been drinking heavily in The Star and had argued. Ellen was sentenced to death, but the sentence was commuted. As a child I recall being shown the blood-stained floorboards, merely covered by a small rug — next to the pottery jerry — such was the rustic simplicity of the home.

The Workhouse
A view taken from above Hunger Hill cottages looking over the Union Workhouse *c.*1910. On the previous page the entrance gateway to the Workhouse can be seen spurring off from Union Street.

Silver Street

Two similar views of Silver Street twenty years apart: the top photograph *c.*1900, but definitely before 1903 as the old Star Inn is still standing. The bottom view was taken either in 1922 or 1923, with the Victoria Hall and Temperance Hotel now having become the town's first cinema.

The Movies Come to Town

The top photograph can be dated to late 1922 or early 1923. One of the posters advertising films lists *Paid Back*, a Hollywood silent movie released in the USA on 28 August 1922.

Before the Bulldozer
London and Manchester
House prior to its demolition
as part of the town centre
clearance. Up to the late
1950s the church was
completely hidden by
buildings which ran up the
north-east side of Silver Street,
all the way round to the
Market Place, linking up with
the church gates.

The Junction with Boulton Lane

Silver Street looking west *c.*1910: these two views show how much the street scene has changed and in particular shows how narrow the road was prior to the clearance. Originally a bypass was planned up Henlow drive and the Slade and as a result much clearance took place in the mid-1950s, but nothing came of this road and in the end it was the town centre which became victim to clearance.

The Market House

This is one of Dursley's saving graces. It was built in 1738 by the Estcourt family of Shipton Moyne who held the lordship of the manor. It was built as an investment to collect tolls, a right jealously guarded by the family leading to disputes in the 1830s. The family finally sold the Market House and its rights to Henry Vizard of Dursley in 1841. The Market House was later managed by a trust, and since 1996 by Dursley Town Council.

The First Petrol Station

The quality of the top photograph print is very poor, but it is included because of its interest. It is one of the earliest pictures in the book and dates from the 1870s. The shop which now houses Bailey's News and the Post Office was built in 1897 by ironmonger Palmer Harding. He was the first person to sell petrol in Dursley, so this was the town's first filling station!

From the Church Tower

These fine views looking south and west are taken from the church tower *c.*1910. In the bottom view the Workhouse can be seen top right, and the Dursley Steam Brewery centre left.

The Market Place

A photograph of the top of Long Street where it meets the Market Place, *c*.1935. By the position of the sun and with cyclists appearing, it must be 12:00, dinner time for the Lister workmen. In the 1960s and 1970s the newly created church wall was a favourite lunchtime seating spot for the Lister apprentices.

Dursley in 1967
This aerial view shows R. A. Lister & Company at its zenith, from here on it was a slow decline.

The valley is completely filled with industry and top left may be seen a corner of the Grammar School and the Gas Works at Trolleymoors.

Long Street circa 1905

The building on the right was originally the New Bell Inn, and later in the nineteenth century became Whitmore's printing office and stamp office. In a 'heliotype' print of 1877 the site covered by W. H. Smith & Son and the Conservative Club (now all of it the Conservative Club) was a walled garden leading to the churchyard, but the site had previously been built on and housed the Golden Hart.

A View Down Long Street

Owen Modes was a very modern shop-front for this postcard view of *c*.1900. It was unusual at this time to have plate glass frontage. By the 1940s the shop had been enlarged at the back and housed F. W. Woolworth, but this had closed by 1970 and the shop is now the Fish Bar.

Long Street Court

A view of Long Street *c.*1900 showing Long Street Court, demolished in the early 1960s to make way for the printing and newspaper works of F. Bailey & Son. Bottom right the house visible to the right of the Priory was demolished in 1910 to make way for Lister offices, but these, in turn, were demolished in 2004, and the lower picture shows the site a few weeks before the bulldozers arrived.

Ashton Lister's Workforce

The Lister workforce *c.*1913 with hardly a bare head in sight. My grandfather, Joseph Sutton, is third from left with a pipe. I think it is a staged photograph to mark some celebration or for a publicity publication. The only similarity between these two views is the storm water drain, its position unchanged for one hundred years.

The End of The Chantry

Another demolition picture, this time the medieval chantry, much of which was demolished in 1935 to make way for the R. A. Lister Social Club. The picture below is Water Street in 2004 with artistic graffiti advertising that 'Mark ——— is sexy'.

One of Ashton Lister's Machine Shops
The separator machine shop, 1938. Below, a view of the separator machine shop area shortly before demolition in 2004.

From Orchard to Industry

A view of Dursley in 1904: an interesting photograph showing some of the early industrial buildings in Water Street. Across the lane, and the Ewelme, leading to Goody Mead the area appears to be covered by kitchen gardens. The colour photograph of May 2004 shows some of this same area prior to clearance.

Goody Mead
Two views one hundred years apart. This area marked the furthest eastward spread of the R. A. Lister works.

A View From The Woods

This interesting photograph shows the town *c.*1905. The new Lister separator machine shop is under construction. The Alexandra Cream Separator was one of Ashton Lister's greatest commercial triumphs. During the 1890s the product won numerous awards and it was probably this single product which

formed the solid foundation of the business which later turned predominantly to engine manufacture. Also in this photograph note the size of London House, bounding the Market Place between Market Hall and Church, also carpets on 'tenter hooks' at Champion's works. Bloodworth's builder's yard in Parsonage Street is clearly visible in the foreground.

From Ashton Lister's Eyrie

This photograph has been reproduced
several times before, but is of interest
for Dursley's industrial heritage. It
appears to have been taken from the
Towers, and as the Dursley Council
School has not yet been built, it must
date from 1897 or 1898.

At this time Howard's mill was
occupied by J. Peake & Company,
timber importers. This building was
demolished and replaced in 1903,
becoming Ashton Lister's Churn Works.
The old Lister foundry buildings are
to the left of the picture. A corner
of Rock House is in the foreground,
mainly obscured by trees. Rock House
had been built in 1865 by one of
Dursley's other major manufacturers,
Edward Gazard. It was named 'Rock
House' because it was built of tufa, and
presumably built over the exhausted
tufa rock quarry bed for which Dursley
had been famed through the centuries.

Industrial Ambitions

An artist's impression of the proposed Lister works, based on a photograph, produced in 1935. Rock House can be seen here and was presumably demolished about this time. The colour photograph shows the sad remains of one of Ashton Lister's early buildings, now (May 2004) empty and awaiting demolition.

Dursley Station

A tank engine slowly reverses into Dursley Station *c.*1900. The line had been built in 1856 by local promoters, but was not initially a commercial success and was taken over by the Midland Railway. The last passenger train steamed out of the station on 10 September 1962, and I was one of the passengers! The line finally closed for goods traffic in 1966.

The bottom photograph is possibly the oldest image in the book, and may date back to 1860. Note the platform is lower by about one foot and that the station went through some remodelling between 1860 and 1900.

The Midland Railway Staff at Dursley

This photograph is probably 1904 as the Heysham terminal and port was opened in that year. In 1902 Midland Railway changed their uniform, the kepi went out and the flatter cap came in. The young man front left is wearing the older kepi, and most of the staff in the back row the new style cap. The guard, second from the right at the back, was Henry Johnson, he worked for the Midland, then the LMS until 23 October 1928 when he was killed in the Charfield rail disaster.

The Centenary

The Dursley branch centenary, 1956. As a boy in the 1950s I often managed to hitch rides in the cab from Dursley to Coaley Junction and back. One quickly got to know which drivers were friendly and willing to break the rules! The key was for the station master not to be around. Being in the cab, throwing coal into the fire and blowing the whistle were huge treats. Imagine the health and safety furore if this was done today.

Sheep Shear

The entrance to Dursley Station yard *c*.1915. In 1923 the Midland Railway was subsumed into the newly created London Midland and Scottish Railway. The factory behind is part of R. A. Lister & Co. On 27 July 1983 a huge fire burnt down the Lister offices and much of the surrounding factory space, and most of this range of factory space was destroyed, the surviving buildings house Lister Shearing Equipment Limited, now a separate company, but still occupying the site where it has been producing shearing equipment for exactly one hundred years — 1908 being the year in which Ashton Lister first marketed shearing equipment.

The New Foundry, 1938

Note the artistic touch-up at the front of the photograph. Originally there were several cottages in the valley by the old mill pond, and one semi-detached pair is still standing in this photograph. Later versions of this same picture have the cottages air-brushed out and the actual date of demolition is unknown. The Foundry covered the site of what had been Oaklands Millpond in the nineteenth century.

The New Recreation Ground

A fair on the Recreation Ground, c.1925, taken from high up in the woods. The equivalent picture is impossible to obtain today due to tree cover. Note that only one house has been built along the Knapp, and that at the eastern end no lime trees (or any trees for that matter) are standing. The remainder of the Knapp appears to host some fine elms. Also note the cottage to the left of the Lister factory, soon to be demolished. The River Cam is unfortunately just out of view, but this led into Oaklands Millpond.

The 'Rec'

A festival on the Recreation Ground *c.*1910. Garden Suburb has not yet been built and also note the tree line on Stinchcombe Hill, behind, without trees at the higher reaches of the woodland.

Castle Farm

A photograph taken early in 1959, just before the demolition of the old police station and courts, which are visible in the background. The farm appears to have been vacated and the field is now a sad sea of docks and other weeds. Up until 1958 cows were walked twice daily down Parsonage Street to the milking parlour in the farm.

Inset: the town centre end of the Knapp *c*.1935.

The End of Castle Farm

The Castle Farm site in 1962 with road-works in full swing. The Market House bypass was done in two stages, the first stage with the road entering Parsonage Street where Barclays Bank now stands. Some three years later there was further demolition at the top of Parsonage Street creating a gap by the side of the Post Office, and the bypass was then extended to this point.

Inset: Herbert Wood sat in his back garden at Castle Farm.

Castle Farm Entrance
The Bell and Castle Hotel on a wet day, *c.*1900. Note the road was unmade at this time with the rain turning it into a muddy thoroughfare.

Inset: Some of the Wood and Vigus families with friends outside The Bell and Castle.

The King's Head and The Old Post Office
Parsonage Street *c.*1905. Note the poor condition of The Kings Head. This building lasted another thirty years and was then replaced with the pub currently standing. In fact, from the Market House right up to Barclays Bank most of these properties have been replaced.

Parsonage Street

This rather grainy photograph from *c.*1915 shows one of the first garages in Dursley. Being next to The Bell and Castle Hotel it was probably run by the Vigus family. The garage later moved to May Lane.

The Bell and Castle

A summer day *c.*1940. The days of mud and dust are now gone with tarmac on the roads. The shop to the right of the Hollies is marked 'Electricity' and was the retail shop of the local electricity company. This became part of the Midlands Electricity Board on nationalisation in 1947, and remained part of the MEB until privatisation in 1990.

Note the cow pats in the road. Were the cows being pastured somewhere the other end of the town? The tree line also deserves attention as it begins to creep down into the field. The height of the trees is also substantially more as scrub and larch are becoming replaced by the more natural beech.

Parsonage Street Before the Use of Tarmac

Parsonage Street *c.*1900. The Hollies in the distance was built in 1733 and was the home and stables of Mr J. M. Buston, haulier and contractor. To the left of this was a farm, demolished *c.*1908 to make way for the new Co-operative Society buildings. On the hillside can be seen a tree line unlike that of today. It appears to be a larch plantation and the felling of this would account for the ability of photographers in the early years of the twentieth century to take some of the views we have seen earlier in this book.

Parsonage Street Looking East

Parsonage Street *c*.1900: a view from the opposite direction taken at about the same time as the photograph on the previous page. Two builders are at work on the roof of The Bell and Castle Hotel, and in an enlargement of this picture they can be seen to be staring at the photographer.

The Narrow Junction of May Lane

Parsonage Street shortly before the building of the new post office, probably c.1938. The Co-operative Café became a butchers shop, but was demolished in the 1960s when May Lane was widened.

A View From Hunger Hill circa 1920
The Regency-styled villa house became
the Black Stallion restaurant in the
1970s and later a popular pub, The
Happy Pig. It was demolished in the
1990s.

Remaining with the pig theme, the
cottages in Hill Road, Hardings Row,
were known locally as 'Pigs Face Row'
as their only door faced to the back,
and not the roadside. Presumably this
meant that the cottagers were facing
their pigs in sties at the bottom of the
small gardens!

Tree growth and much new building
in the area have made any modern
photography virtually impossible.

Hunger Hill circa 1915

A view of the forbidding Dursley Union Workhouse. The manse in the foreground was built for the minister of the local Methodist circuit in 1824 and was sold in 1958. The manse and cottages in Hunger Hill have survived, but everything else has changed beyond recognition. The houses on the workhouse site are rather unfortunate in having a barrack-like appearance. The previously neat workhouse gardens have taken on the form of a scrub-covered bank.

The New Co-op

From the diversion to May Lane the 'Through Time' itinerary returns to Parsonage Street, this time c.1912. The road appears to have been 'macadamised', but there is still no sign of tarmac. Some fifteen years ago, Harry, an old neighbour of mine, related his memory of Drake Lane being tarmac surfaced in the mid 1920s. Apparently the steam rollers did not have the power to go up Drake Lane, so for each 'pass' of rolling they had go via Kingshill Road, Gasworks Pitch, Spring Hill and then down again, each circuit of rolling taking about two hours!

Bottom photograph:
Colyton House, faced the Co-op until it was demolished in 1964.

The Wild Goose Garage

The band leading the Gala Day float procession, 1958. The cottages at the back of the filling station appear to date from c.1760 and were demolished in 1962. The picture below is from c.1969 and shows a style of architecture best forgotten. Petrol in 1969 (in pounds, shillings and pence) was 78d (6s 6d) per gallon. Adjusted for inflation, this equates to 66 pence per litre, whereas, at the time of writing in 2008 the current price is 110 pence per litre – almost double. The price of the average semi-detached house in Dursley at this time was £4,500.

The Promenade

This postcard view of 1905 grandly names Kingshill Road 'the Promenade, Dursley'. Note how narrow the road is at this time, with the footpath being spacious, but like the road, of macadamised surface which would have been dusty in summer and very muddy in winter. To the right was Rednock, the estate of Captain George Augustus Graham (1833-1909).

Inset: Dursley Secondary School first XI 1927-28 with 'Joe' West far right. 'Joe' remained Senior Master until his retirement in 1965, striking fear and respect into all.

Kingshill Road circa 1908

Rednock House had previously been known as Oaklands (some maps call it Oatlands), but on Graham's early retirement from the Indian Army he bought the house and grounds and renamed it Rednock, the name of one of the septs of clan Graham. Septs were families that a clan could regard as loyal, either families related to the clan by blood, or families that obtained protection from the clan. Captain Graham is credited with saving the Irish Wolfhound and the Scottish Deerhound from extinction. It was in 1859, at the age of 26 that he became the owner of his first wolfhound, Faust. From that date he devoted his life to the resuscitation of the breed.

Twelve years after Captain Graham's death, the house was bought for the use of the new Dursley Secondary School. In 1947 it became Dursley Grammar School, with the addition of red brick wings each side of the old house. In 1971 the school merged with Dursley Secondary Modern School to become Rednock, thereby unknowingly re-introducing a Scottish sept name.

Kingshill Road

Top: some of Eddie Wood's cows, led by a goat, on their way down to Castle Farm.

Bottom: an aerial photograph of Kingshill, 1967 with the ABC Regal Cinema centre of view. The development of the cinema, parade of shops and the houses behind — Jubilee Road, Olive Grove, Lawrence Grove etc. were built by Bishopston entrepreneur, Leonard Watts (1897-1963). He started off his building career in Bristol by offering to install lavatories in houses. The Kingshill development was his largest project and was described as 'one of the most magnificent sites in the country' with houses being offered for sale or to rent. Building started in 1935 with the first road being named Jubilee Road from King George V's Silver Jubilee. Olive Grove was named after Len's wife, Olive. Presumably Lawrence was another member of the family.

Kingshill Parade circa 1940

Kingshill Road runs north-west out of Dursley towards Cam and there was no development much further than Garden Suburb until the 1930s. During the First World War the land the woodland side of the road was used by the 5th Glosters as a training area and mock trenches were dug for recruits to experience trench life before departing for the Western Front. The lane running up to Westfield Wood was an actual road until the early part of the twentieth century, but it has now reduced to little more than a footpath. The site now covered by Watts' estate was an orchard and kitchen gardens, possibly nineteenth-century allotments. It also appears to have been used as a rubbish tip area for Dursley refuse in the early nineteenth century.

The Newly Built Kingshill Inn
This photograph appears to have been taken in the final stages of development in 1936. The concrete road looks freshly laid. The licence for the new Kingshill Inn was transferred from The Bull Inn at Woodmancote which had now closed.

Kingshill House, 1900

The house was built in 1706 for the wealthy clothier Thomas Purnell. Between 1825 and 1830 the house appears to have been inherited by Robert John Hooper who in accordance with the will of Lt. Col. Purnell took the surname Purnell. In fact there were two distinguished branches of this clothier Purnell family in Dursley, one branch being at Ferney Hill and at Stancombe Park, the other, and less successful branch, at Kingshill. In the 1850s and 60s the last Purnell was Revd. Thomas Purnell, but it was not a happy home, and in 1856 Purnell attended an inquest to record that his gardener had hanged himself in the hot house. In 1865 the estate was sold to Thomas Richards a successful Dursley malster whose sister Louisa had married George Lister, the father of Robert Ashton Lister. From here, the history gets a bit hazy, for Arthur Ruscombe Poole of Bridgwater, Somerset, became resident, and he was related to a Hooper. It seems possible that Purnell associated family remained in the property as tenants. The house and grounds were eventually bought by Robert Ashton Lister.

Haymaking at Norman Hill

Eddie Wood haymaking at Norman Hill. The Norman Hill estate was owned by Arthur Strachan Winterbotham (1864-1936). He was the son of Arthur Brend Winterbotham, mill owner and M.P. for Cirencester. Arthur senior was one of the founders of Cam Cricket Club. Arthur junior was a distinguished cricketer and played for Gloucestershire. The view was almost impossible to recreate due to the housing on the site. To be on the precise spot today would be to almost stand inside one of the Norman Hill houses.

Haymaking to the West of Sandpits

The Wood Family of Castle Farm used several fields between Dursley and Cam. One area farmed by them was the land between the Grammar School and the Lister Works. This top photograph is taken somewhere to the west of Sandpits.

In the bottom photograph Eddie Wood is posing with a young friend, leaning against a wagon apparently being used for muck-spreading!

Harvesting in the Field Across From The Yew Tree

Eddie Wood of Castle Farm harvesting just across the road from The Yew Tree Inn. Having his farmhouse near the centre of Dursley was inconvenient, but appears to have been enterprising and owned or rented land in various locations, including Norman Hill as we have seen on the previous page. In this instance, the land belonged to family, for Elm House belonged to the Wood Family.

Elm House and the Yew Tree Inn
The Yew Tree Inn bottom right, and the road leading away to Berkeley Road junction c.1905. The road to Stinchcombe (foreground) had some fine mature elm trees which were sadly blighted by Dutch Elm Disease in 1976 and felled shortly afterwards. In this photograph Elm house is the ivy covered house in the foreground.

This view is impossible to reproduce today due to tree growth, but in attempting to do so I did take other photographs showing one of the delights of May time on Stinchcombe Hill — the Purple Orchid.

Not One Bare Head!
A donkey trap excursion *c.*1910 and Dursley Cycle Club, 1907. Being a book primarily of comparisons there is a sad lack of human interest, and it was difficult to leave out these two wonderful images.

The Crossways, Upper Cam circa 1930
The car looks as if it is a 1927 Morris Cowley flatnose, but somehow the top of the radiator is not quite right for me to be sure.

Cam Mills

The main works of Messrs. Hunt & Winterbotham Limited. The Company was formed in 1859 when Thomas Hunt of Cam Mills took in Arthur Brend Winterbotham (1838-1892) as partner. Quite how a 21-year-old had the necessary money seems a surprise. The name Winterbotham sounds as if it originated in Yorkshire, but in fact Arthur had been born in Cambridgeshire, and his father, Lindsey, in Plymouth in 1799. Brend was his grandmother's maiden name. Arthur was a local J.P. and M.P. for Cirencester, 1885-92. He married into another clothier family, taking Elizabeth Strachen as his wife in 1863. The firm of Hunt & Winterbotham still exists and is now based in Huddersfield.

Cam Station circa 1925
The buildings to the left of the station appear to have been absorbed into extra factory extensions shortly after this photograph was taken and still stand today. The station itself closed in 1962 and was soon demolished. I recall as a boy in the 1950s standing on the bridge and watching as the stream turned bright blue or bright red depending which dyes were being discharged on that day — an occurrence almost unimaginable today.

Station Road

Two views of Station Road approximately forty years apart, the top being *c.*1900 and the bottom *c.*1940. This view is probably the least changed throughout this whole book.

The Temperance Hotel

The 'Welcome' coffee tavern and temperance hotel, *c.*1900. The hotel was built in 1896, under the influence of one of Arthur Winterbotham's daughters. The photograph was taken from Red House Farm.

Chapel Street, Lower Cam, circa 1900

The agricultural machine is stood outside the blacksmith shop of Absolom Ford, known as 'Appy Ford'.

In the 1831 census the population of Cam was 2,071, by 2001 this had increased to 8,500. Also, the focus of the village has changed with housing all the way up the hill towards Stinchcombe, whereas in the 1830s it was very much in the valley bottom.

In the colour photograph, note the small piece of surviving cast-iron railing.

Chapel Street, circa 1910
The fine wall bounding the farm yard of White House Farm has long gone to facilitate the widening of the road. The chapel was built in 1825 to serve the local Methodist community. The manse for the chapel was at the bottom of Cam Pitch, at the far left end of this stone wall, but out of view. It later became the local branch of the Cainscross and Ebley Co-operative Society as shown on the following page.

Cam Pitch circa 1910
The vicar and his wife braving the snow. The old vicarage is on the left of the photograph.

Inset: a glimpse of the old manse in its later incarnation as the Co-op, *c.*1959. Note the sunken pathway in front of the shop. This is the point from which the colour view was photographed.

Lower Cam High Street circa 1900
There is much change over the past hundred years. St Bartholomew's and the thatched cottage survive, although the latter has been transmogrified. All of the other properties have been demolished and replaced, including the row of cottages known as Troytown.

The Jubilee Green circa 1902

The Jubilee Tree is the key to dating here, for it was planted in 1897 to celebrate Queen Victoria's Diamond Jubilee. Here it looks as if it is about five years old.

In the colour photograph the semi-detached houses are hidden, but the cottages on the right-hand side are a rare survival.

High Street, Lower Cam circa 1935

A Red and White bus is parked outside The Berkeley Arms and a herd of cows is making its way down to White House Farm for milking. By the position of the sun this is the afternoon rather than the morning milking. It always fascinated me as a child watching the cows go into Castle Farm in Dursley. There was rarely anyone supervising, the cows knew exactly where to go and what to do. For the few minutes they were in the street, people and cars stopped and waited, for cows have minds of their own.

The Northend, High Street, Lower Cam circa 1945

There is little obvious change here apart from the increased vegetation and the dramatic increase in motor vehicles. The telegraph poles have gone, but lamp standards and other poles have increased. The electricity supply pole looks the same, but is probably a replacement in the same place.

Draycott circa 1935
Workman Brothers flour silos dominate the landscape in the old picture.

Draycott Mill circa 1910

A more gentle scene, two horse wagons in the front, but in the back are two steam wagons, building up steam before making their deliveries.

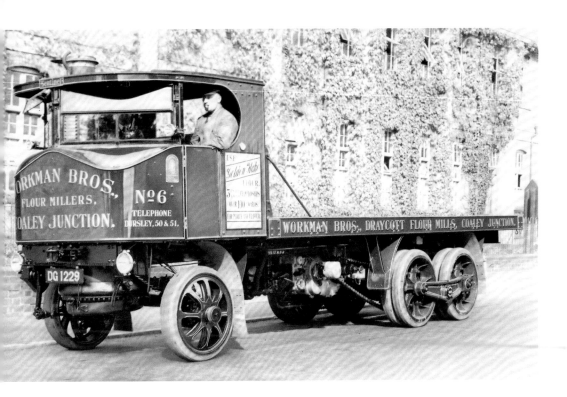

Steam Power

Workman Brothers were great believers in steam powered lorries. This photograph of the early 1930s shows a 1931 Sentinel DG6, presumably when it had just been delivered from the Sentinel works in Shrewsbury. The bottom photograph shows Draycott Mill in 1967.

Coaley Junction

This magnificent photograph, *c.*1904, was probably taken at the same time as that on page 49, when the Midland Railway uniform was going through its change. The Station Master and guard look familiar from the earlier views.

Cambridge circa 1910

'Eves', bakers, confectioners and light refreshments. Cambridge was the junction of the main road to Dursley until the M5 was built, after which the junction moved half a mile south to the Slimbridge crossroads. A turnpike stood at the old Wisloe crossroads. Cambridge was also an important coaching stop for the change of post horses before the advent of the railways.

The George Inn

Together with The White Lion, the inn served as a coaching inn with post horses. Although not as important as Newport, four miles south, it did have much trade on the main Gloucester to Bristol route. Most trade fell away with the coming of the railway in the 1840s. The road was originally a Roman road and in winter Cambridge was frequently subject to bad flooding.